What's It Like Out?
Forecasting!

Kris Hirschmann

ABDO
Publishing Company

visit us at
www.abdopublishing.com

Published by ABDO Publishing Company, 8000 West 78th Street, Edina, Minnesota 55439.
Copyright © 2008 by Abdo Consulting Group, Inc. International copyrights reserved in all
countries. No part of this book may be reproduced in any form without written permission from the
publisher. The Checkerboard Library™ is a trademark and logo of ABDO Publishing Company.

Printed in the United States.

Cover Photo: AP Images
Interior Photos: Alamy p. 19; AP Images pp. 1, 14, 26; Comstock pp. 17, 29; Getty Images pp. 5, 7,
    25, 27; iStockphoto pp. 11, 21; National Oceanic and Atmospheric Administration/Department
    of Commerce pp. 10, 17; PhotoEdit pp. 9, 23, 28; Photo Researchers, Inc. p. 12; U.S. Coast
    Guard p. 13

Series Coordinator: Megan M. Gunderson
Editors: Rochelle Baltzer, Megan M. Gunderson
Art Direction & Cover Design: Neil Klinepier

Library of Congress Cataloging-in-Publication Data

Hirschmann, Kris, 1967-
  Forecasting! / Kris Hirschmann.
      p. cm. -- (What's it like out?)
  Includes bibliographical references and index.
  ISBN 978-1-59928-941-0
  1. Weather forecasting--Juvenile literature. I. Title.

  QC995.43.H57 2008
  551.63--dc22

                            2007029158

Contents

100 Percent Chance of Weather

Imagine you're getting ready to leave for school. You look out the window and see gray skies. "I wonder if I should take an umbrella?" you think.

To answer this question, you turn on the television. You flip to a local news channel and watch the weather report. "There is a 90 percent chance of rain today," says the forecaster. That's just what you needed to know! On your way out the door, you grab your umbrella and your raincoat.

Predicting the weather is important for more than just our daily lives. The weather affects crop planting schedules, airplane flights, international trade, military plans, and the cost of food. Extreme weather events such as tornadoes and hurricanes can harm people and property. Weather forecasts help us make good choices when these things happen.

Weather affects the food we buy. For example, cold temperatures in Florida or California can raise the price of the oranges.

Watching the Skies

People have been **predicting** the weather for thousands of years. Ancient forecasters paid attention to daily conditions because it was important for safety and finding food. They used these observations along with past experiences to make guesses about future conditions. This included predicting rain, wind, and other changes in weather.

Many old weather guesses survive today as proverbs, or folk sayings. These sayings do not always correctly predict the weather. But, some proverbs do have a grain of truth. For instance, "Red sky at night, sailor's delight. Red sky at morning, sailors take warning," is often **accurate**.

Red skies at night often mean sunlight is passing through clear skies in the west. Since weather often travels west to east, this means clear weather is on its way. Red skies in the morning often mean clear skies in the east and clouds in the west. This could indicate stormy weather is approaching.

People have also relied on animals and insects for weather forecasting. If a groundhog sees its shadow on Groundhog Day, many people believe there will be six more weeks of winter. Cattle lying in a field may mean they are saving a dry place because rain is on the way. Other people believe rain is coming if ants build tall entrances around their nests.

People have used red skies to forecast weather for thousands of years.

Early Progress

Folk sayings may have been useful for **predicting** weather. But they were also mysterious. Long ago, no one really understood how weather worked.

Greek philosopher Aristotle tried to figure it out. Around 350 BC, Aristotle wrote a book called *Meteorologica*. This book explains clouds and other weather events. Aristotle's explanations were not all correct, but they were still important. They gave people a new way to think about the weather.

Centuries later, scientists started creating tools to measure weather. In 1593, Italian scientist Galileo invented the thermometer to measure temperature. In 1644, Italian scientist Evangelista Torricelli described the mercury barometer. This weather invention measures atmospheric pressure. Now, scientists could collect real weather measurements.

The development of the electric **telegraph** in 1837 was another important advancement in forecasting. It let people

U.S. WEATHER MAP

Lightning
Temperatures
Jet Stream
Sunny
Warm Front
Cold Front
Tornado
Tropical Storm
Hurricane
Cloud
Rain
Sleet
Snow
L Low
H High

*To create a synoptic map, weather
conditions are observed at the same time
over a large area and compiled.*

communicate weather data across long distances. When
they did, they could make **synoptic** maps. Soon, people
could see large-scale weather patterns. A new age of
weather forecasting was about to begin.

Moving into the Modern Era

The science of meteorology has changed a lot since the 1800s. Today, scientists have more **accurate** thermometers and barometers. They also have easier ways to communicate. And, other new tools such as **radar** and **satellites** help them better understand local and global weather.

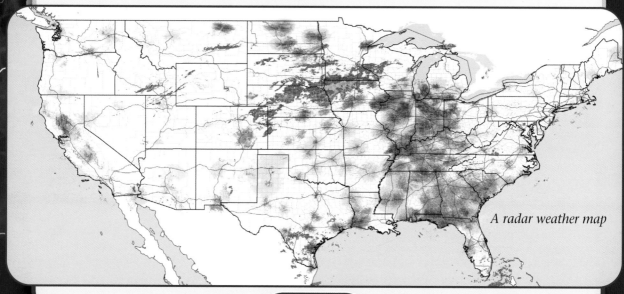

A radar weather map

Today, aerovanes often combine the duties of anemometers and weather vanes. This airplane-shaped instrument has a propeller at the front that measures wind speed. The aerovane's tail lines up the device with the wind to indicate direction.

Some of these tools collect information about an immediate area. For example, rain **gauges** measure rainfall. Anemometers (a-nuh-MAH-muh-tuhrs) measure wind speed, while weather vanes indicate wind direction. Hygrometers measure humidity, which is the amount of moisture in the air.

Other tools collect weather information from a distance. **Radar** devices create images of faraway storms. **Satellites** take pictures of storm systems from high above Earth. And, powerful computers receive and combine weather data from many areas at once. Using these tools, meteorologists can study weather occurring anywhere on the planet.

Local Conditions

To measure local conditions, meteorologists use weather stations. Some stations are staffed, while others **automatically** transmit data.

At weather stations, thermometers, barometers, and hygrometers are put into special slatted boxes called Stevenson screens. The slats let some air enter these instrument shelters. But they block strong winds, rain, and direct sunlight. This protects the instruments and helps them take **accurate** readings.

Stevenson screens are painted white to reflect sunlight. They are placed 4 feet (1.2 m) above the ground to allow air to circulate.

Other weather station tools are located in the open. Anemometers and weather vanes are placed in wide-open areas, where wind blows freely. Rain **gauges** work best in relatively open areas. So, scientists set them apart from anything that might block rain. But, rain gauges should not be in areas where strong winds could affect the readings.

Numerous buoys and ships collect and transmit weather data at sea.

Radar is also useful for collecting local data. These devices can be set up almost anywhere. Permanent radar units may sit high off the ground on towers. Smaller, mobile units can be moved from place to place. Scientists use both fixed and mobile radar instruments to track weather systems.

Weather on a Large Scale

It is important to understand local weather. But this is just part of an **accurate** forecast. To **predict** future conditions, meteorologists must also look at larger weather patterns.

Sending up weather balloons is one way to do this. A small instrument package called a radiosonde (RAY-dee-oh-sahnd) is attached to each balloon. As the balloons go up, the radiosondes collect data.

This data includes air temperature, atmospheric pressure, and humidity. Scientists also use **radar** to track the balloons. This tells them the speed and direction of high-level winds. Radiosonde data is collected and shared worldwide.

Airplanes gather data as well. High-flying commercial airplanes carry weather sensors. These instruments give scientists a great deal of information about global weather conditions.

For an even bigger view, scientists rely on **satellites**. Satellite photos clearly show clouds, hurricanes, and other weather systems from above. They let us see things that people could only guess at in the recent past.

Worldwide, weather balloons are launched at the same time twice a day, every day of the year. More than 1,500 take weather measurements daily! The balloon bursts at a high altitude, and then a parachute guides the radiosonde down again. If found, a radiosonde can be rebuilt and reused as one of the 75,000 the National Weather Service launches every year!

Sharing Weather

All weather data is important. Local information tells us about large-scale systems. Meanwhile, global patterns help us **predict** local conditions. Weather doesn't stop at one nation's border. To help make **accurate** forecasts, this information must be relayed to meteorologists all over the world.

The United Nations' World Meteorological Organization (WMO) makes sure global weather data is collected and **distributed**. More than 180 nations and territories collect weather data at certain times every day.

That data is **compiled** at three world meteorological centers. There, computers **analyze** the data and determine forecasts. Scientists everywhere can then access the data.

Weather data also is compiled at national offices. In the United States, the central weather organization is the National Weather Service (NWS). It is part of the National Oceanic and Atmospheric Administration (NOAA).

You can see local forecasts on a computer by visiting one of NOAA's Web sites. Visit often to see if their computers and forecasters are accurate!

The National Weather Service uses one of the fastest supercomputers in the world to continue improving its forecasts. It can compile 240 million global observations every day!

At the NWS's National Meteorological Center near Washington, D.C., computers and meteorologists use data sent in by weather stations nationwide to create forecasts. These **predictions** are then sent to local NWS forecast offices and centers.

Short-Term Predictions

After data has been collected, it is **analyzed**. One of a meteorologist's main jobs is to make short-term **predictions**. In other words, he or she must forecast the weather for the coming hours and days.

Sometimes forecasters use the steady-state, or trend, **technique**. They do this if a weather system's behavior is constant. For example, a system may be moving at a steady speed. Or, its temperature may be changing at a certain rate. Steady-state forecasts assume that these trends will continue.

Today, meteorologists rely on computer forecasts. To make predictions, a computer runs weather data through sets of **equations** called models. It mathematically determines what the weather will be like in ten minutes. Then, it runs this new set of conditions through the equations again. By repeating this process, computers can predict the weather far into the future.

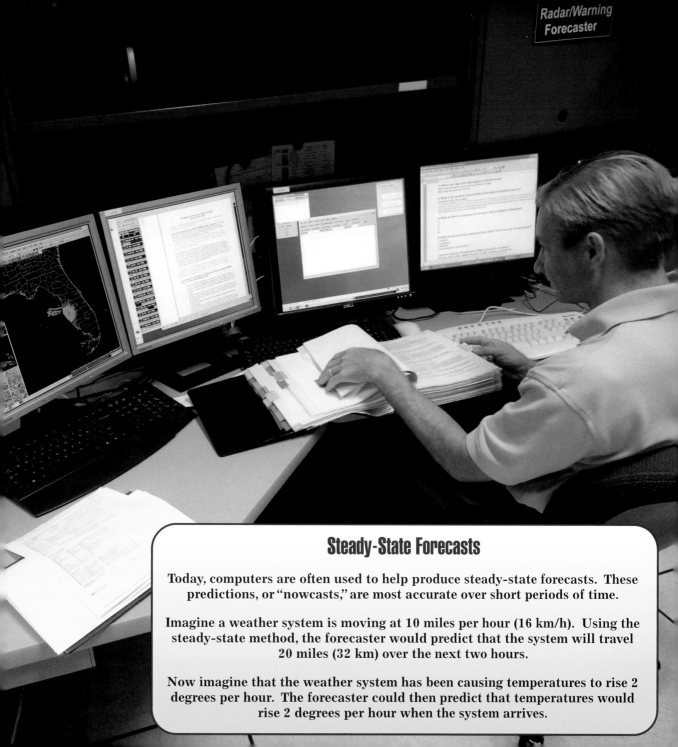

Steady-State Forecasts

Today, computers are often used to help produce steady-state forecasts. These predictions, or "nowcasts," are most accurate over short periods of time.

Imagine a weather system is moving at 10 miles per hour (16 km/h). Using the steady-state method, the forecaster would predict that the system will travel 20 miles (32 km) over the next two hours.

Now imagine that the weather system has been causing temperatures to rise 2 degrees per hour. The forecaster could then predict that temperatures would rise 2 degrees per hour when the system arrives.

An Inexact Science

Computers can use current data to **predict** conditions for any date. In theory, you could press a button and check next year's weather! But in reality, weather forecasting doesn't work that way.

Weather data is never 100 percent correct to start with. And, conditions that affect weather are always changing. So eventually, the **equations** produce wrong answers. The errors increase each time the computer crunches the numbers.

For this reason, meteorologists use **probabilities** to describe weather. For example, they might calculate that there is a 50 percent chance of rain. A percentage may also be based on the amount of an area expected to get **precipitation**. Stable weather conditions can lead to higher percentages.

The **accuracy** of a computer forecast depends on the time frame. A forecast for the next 12 hours is probably excellent. A one-day prediction exceeds 90 percent accuracy, which is still good. And a two-day forecast is still substantial.

Five-day **predictions** may seem like reasonable guesses. But, they are as good as three-day forecasts were in the 1980s. Any prediction beyond this point is just a guideline. Conditions will almost certainly change as the days pass.

A typical forecast for your area might predict temperature highs and lows, wind speeds, the probability of rain, and how cloudy the skies will be.

SEVEN-DAY FORECAST

THU	FRI	SAT	SUN	MON	TUE	WED
HOT!		40%		windy	80%	
96	90	85	82	89	78	85
70	67	72	69	76	61	65
S 15-25	S 10-20	E 10-15	SE 10-15	SE 20-30	S 5-10	S 10-20

Putting It All Together

One-day computer forecasts are **accurate** about 85 percent of the time. That's not bad. But meteorologists can use their experience and training to complete the weather picture.

To fine-tune a forecast, a meteorologist compares several computer **predictions**. Each prediction uses slightly different data. If the predictions agree, they are probably correct. With this information, the meteorologist could make a forecast without looking any further.

But sometimes, computer predictions do not agree. They indicate many possible conditions. When this happens, meteorologists must dig deeper. They may look at **satellite** pictures or maps. They may also consider an area's geography. For example, mountains and lakes may affect local weather in ways the computer did not consider.

Finally, meteorologists turn to personal experience. They think about an area's weather history. They use all of this information to decide what they think will happen in the coming days. Then, they can finally make a **prediction**!

Meteorologists combine computer predictions, current conditions, and their own experience to bring you the forecast on television nightly.

Long-Term Forecasts

Meteorologists do not just make short-term **predictions**. They make long-term forecasts, too. These forecasts address temperature trends, the likelihood of **precipitation**, and other climate issues. For this reason, they are sometimes called climatological (kleye-muh-tuh-LAH-jih-kuhl) forecasts.

Some long-term forecasts take a persistence approach. This means they assume that current conditions will last. For example, someone might say that a warm spring means a warm summer. These predictions are only sometimes true. They work best in areas where the weather does not change much from day to day.

The analog approach is more scientific. When using this approach, the current year's weather is compared to past years. Scientists use the most similar past year to forecast

Weather trends are very important in agriculture. Long-term forecasts help farmers make the right choices about crops and planting schedules. By doing so, they prevent many costly mistakes.

the rest of the current year's weather. Still, these forecasts are only partly reliable.

Today, persistence and analog approaches are seldom used. Most modern scientists study the oceans instead. They base their long-term forecasts on ocean currents and water temperatures. For example, if the seas are warmer than usual, scientists **predict** stormy periods in certain areas.

Emergency Forecasts

Tornadoes, hurricanes, blizzards, and other severe weather events can be very dangerous. Whenever possible, people must know exactly what these systems are going to do. So, meteorologists work together to make the most **accurate** forecast possible.

As part of NOAA, the NWS is in charge of emergency forecasting in the United States. Its Storm **Prediction** Center tracks tornadoes

Watches are issued when severe weather events are likely. Warnings are issued when severe weather has already formed or will be arriving soon.

and severe thunderstorms. NOAA's National Hurricane Center tracks hurricanes.

NOAA's scientists use advanced equipment to study severe weather. Together, they forecast where storms are more likely to occur. Then, the meteorologists release these forecasts to the public through the **media**. Today, the Internet, including the NWS's Web site, is another vital source for storm information.

The National Hurricane Center produces forecasts and issues warnings to keep as many people safe from severe weather as possible.

The Future of Forecasting

Scientists are just starting to understand how the seas affect our climate. As they learn more every year, they make better long-term forecasts. This trend will continue if people keep studying the oceans.

Approximately 90 percent of people consult weather forecasts one to two times per day.

Short-term forecasting is improving as well. Computer programs are constantly being **upgraded**. As a result, they are becoming more **accurate**.

Satellites are helping meteorologists become more accurate, too. Today, more weather satellites circle the earth than ever before. Some of them take pictures of weather systems. Others study our planet's changing climate.

For example, NASA satellites named Terra, Aqua, and Aura are weather "eyes in the sky." They watch the earth's atmosphere, temperature, moisture, rainfall, and more. Using these and other tools, scientists hope to become even more successful at forecasting!

Glossary

accurate - free of errors.

analyze - to determine the meaning of something by breaking down its parts.

automatic - something that happens by itself, without anyone's control.

compile - to collect or bring together items into one place.

distribute - to give out or deliver something to each individual in a group.

equation - a mathematical statement showing equality between two elements, often using an equal sign. A statement such as $1+1=2$ is an equation.

gauge - a measuring device.

media - a form or system of communication, information, or entertainment that includes television, radio, and newspapers.

precipitation - moisture such as rain, hail, or snow that falls to Earth.

predict - to guess something ahead of time on the basis of observation, experience, or reasoning.

probability - a measure of how likely something is to occur.

radar - a device that sends out and receives the reflections of radio waves, often used for detecting the location or speed of things.

satellite - a manufactured object that orbits Earth. It relays weather and scientific information back to Earth.

synoptic - displaying meteorological data from many observations taken at the same time over a large area.

technique - a method or style in which something is done.

telegraph - a device that uses electricity to send coded messages over wires.

upgrade - to increase or improve.

Web Sites

To learn more about weather, visit ABDO Publishing Company on the World Wide Web at **www.abdopublishing.com**. Web sites about weather are featured on our Book Links page. These links are routinely monitored and updated to provide the most current information available.

Index